emily cier

PIXEL
play

15 Quilt Projects
for Kids, Family & Home

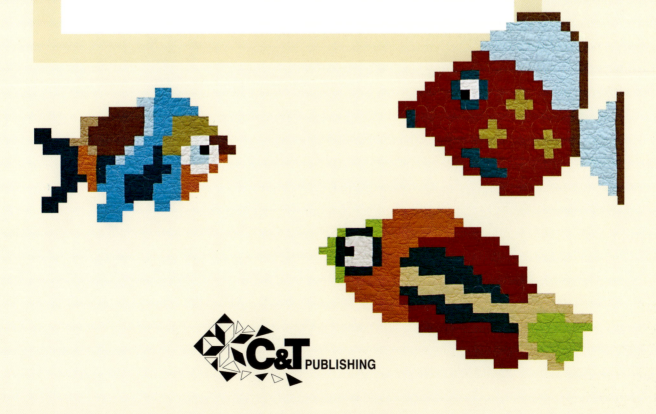

C&T PUBLISHING

Text and Artwork copyright © 2012 by Emily Cier

Photography and Artwork copyright © 2012 by C&T Publishing, Inc.

Publisher: Amy Marson

Creative Director: Gailen Runge

Art Director: Kristy Zacharias

Editor: Liz Aneloski

Technical Editor: Ann Haley

Cover/Book Designer: April Mostek

Production Coordinator: Jenny Davis

Production Editor: Alice Mace Nakanishi

Illustrator: Emily Cier

Photography by Christina Carty-Francis and Diane Pedersen of C&T Publishing, Inc., unless otherwise noted

Published by C&T Publishing, Inc., P.O. Box 1456, Lafayette, CA 94549

Library of Congress Cataloging-in-Publication Data

Cier, Emily.

Pixel play : 15 quilt projects for kids, family & home / Emily Cier.

    p. cm.

ISBN 978-1-60705-358-3 (soft cover)

1. Patchwork--Patterns. 2. Quilting--Patterns. 3. Patchwork quilts. I. Title.

TT835.C4984 2012

746.46--dc23

                              2011052456

Printed in China

10 9 8 7 6 5 4 3 2 1

dedication

For Maeve and Liam
My 24-bit inspirations for these 8-bit quilts.

acknowledgments

Sean
For being there for me through every step of the way.
You are truly the most quilt-literate software engineer
who has never sewn a quilt.

Maeve and Liam
For oohing and aahing at all of Mommy's creations.
The love you have for all your quilts makes my heart melt.
To you two, everything that is a pixel is a quilt, and all quilts
are made of pixels.

Everyone at C&T Publishing
Especially Amy, Gailen, Susanne, Liz, Ann, April, Jenny, and Alice—
for giving me the opportunity to write yet another book.

Robert Kaufman Fabrics
For providing box after box of glorious Kona Cotton for the quilts.

Cathy Kirk
For your impeccable quilting.

P3K
Without you, I'd have a lot more gray hair.

CONTENTS

PIXEL PLAY

04

INTRODUCTION

My kids love all the quilts I make, but never as much as when they know that the quilt I'm working on is for them. They go so far as to request their favorite character or obsession of the month—my son's first and biggest gift request each birthday and holiday is for a new cartoon quilt, and it's difficult to even find my daughter's bed under all her princess quilts and flower pillows.

Sure, they like abstract and geometric patterns, bright new color schemes, and fun shapes. But nothing brings delight to kids' eyes like a scene they can recognize and relate to—and yes, obsess over—crafted into their very own quilt.

To this end, I've learned that the pixel technique is my best friend when it comes to quilts for my family. It's the perfect marriage of simplicity and flexibility. Countless millions of different shapes and scenes can be built from simple strips and squares, yet require sewing only straight lines.

There's something about the impressionistic look of a few dozen squares suddenly resolving into a complete scene that makes me just want to stare at a pixel quilt and smile. I hope these quilts have the same effect on you and your family!

Photo by Emily Cier

Photo by Emily Cier

ONE STRIP AT A TIME:
a pixel quilting primer

fabric, thread, and supplies

The quilts in *Pixel Play* use Robert Kaufman's Kona Cotton Solids (sold in quilt shops and online). The exact color used for each fabric is noted in the yardage charts.

Can I use different Kona colors from those listed?
What about fabrics from a different manufacturer?

Certainly! I've loved Kona Cottons since I began quilting, so they are always my go-to fabrics when making quilts from solids. Many other beautiful solids are available, so feel free to experiment. I do advise picking out all the colors and evaluating the entire palette together before finalizing alternate Kona colors or those from another manufacturer. Having the wrong shade of just one color can throw off the entire palette of the quilt.

A lot of different fabrics are used.
Can I reduce the number of colors?

Not really. I've reduced the number of colors as much as possible. The goal is to allow details to show, while not using every color manufactured.

Can I use a completely different palette?

Of course! I've included alternative palettes for five of the projects: *Fishbowl* Crib (page 19); *Dithered* Crib (page 23); *Snowflakes* Throw (page 47); *Fishbowl* Twin (page 73); and *Dithered* Twin (page 78).

You can also start from scratch and pick your own palette. Start with a color that catches your eye and build from there. I cut up a Kona Cotton Solids color card (available online) into little color chips to help with this. You can use the Kona chips in conjunction with the Ultimate 3-in-1 Color Tool and Studio Color Wheel (both by C&T Publishing) to help build alternative palettes for these quilts or any other projects that use solids.

Photo by Emily Cier

Fishbowl **Twin (pages 68 and 73), shown in both color palettes**

Can I use prints?

Prints probably aren't the best choice for these quilts. There's just too much contrast within the fabric to form a coherent pixel quilt. The exception would be textured solids, which would work fine.

Should I use a certain thread?

I use a cotton 50-weight thread. Thin thread is essential for this technique because the large number of seams will build up even more bulk with thick thread.

Do I need any additional supplies?

You don't need anything special to make pixel quilts beyond your basic quilting supplies. The following are some basic tools I find handy:

- *24˝ × 36˝ cutting mat*

- *Rotary cutter and extra blades:* If you can't remember the last time you replaced your blade or if you find yourself sawing through fabric, it's (past) time to replace your blade.

- *6˝ × 24˝ cutting ruler:* For cutting the long width-of-fabric (WOF) strips

- *4½˝ square cutting ruler:* For cutting the smaller squares from the WOF strips. This ruler is large enough to get a secure grip but small enough that it's not unwieldy to use.

- *Water-soluble pen:* This can come in handy for some of the quilting options (page 12). I keep two pens around: blue for light-colored fabrics and white for dark-colored fabrics.

STEP 1: cutting

1. Iron all fabrics. I prefer not to prewash my fabrics because I feel that the small pieces keep their shapes better when they have not been washed, but it's up to you. Please note that the fabric yardage requirements given for each project do not allow for significant shrinkage due to prewashing.

2. For each color, cut the number of 1½˝ × WOF strips listed in the *First cut* section of each cutting chart.

3. In the *Second cut* section, start by taking a strip from the previous step and subcut. Start with the longest subcut; then cut the longest remaining subcut possible from the leftover portion until the strip is too small to be useful.

4. Continue with the remaining strips until all subcuts for that fabric have been made.

5. Repeat Steps 2–4 with the remaining colors.

Cutting Notes

- All cuts assume that the fabric is at least 40˝ wide. The cutting instructions include one extra strip, and the yardage requirements include enough for a couple extra strips in case of a cutting error.

- For strips longer than 40˝ wide, sew two WOF strips together end-to-end and then subcut, starting with the longest pieces.

- It's best to cut all of the pieces for the quilt before you start sewing. It's no fun to get to row 5 and realize you need to cut more fabric.

- To keep your fabrics organized, stack all the pieces from a single color in a pile with the largest pieces on the bottom.

- Line up the piles in alphabetical order next to your sewing machine.

- Place a piece of paper with the color letter next to each stack of fabrics for easy referencing when piecing. This is especially helpful when there are multiple shades of a single color.

STEP 2:
strip assembly

Chain piecing is the simplest way to sew the strips.

1. Following the quilt assembly diagram, sew Piece 1 to Piece 2, Piece 3 to Piece 4, Piece 5 to Piece 6, and so on.

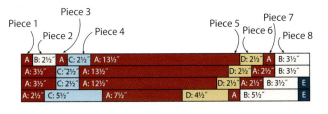

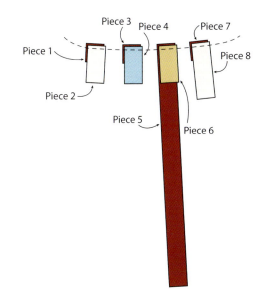

2. Snip the thread between each unit.

3. Continue chain piecing by sewing Unit 1/2 to Unit 3/4, Unit 5/6 to Unit 7/8, and so on.

4. Snip and continue to sew units together until you have completed the entire strip.

5. Set the strip aside until all the strips for that section are complete and then continue with Step 3: Quilt Top Assembly (page 10).

Strip Assembly Notes

■ A ¼″ seam allowance is used for all seams in all of the projects. It's a good idea to do a test seam before you begin sewing to check that your ¼″ seam is accurate. Accuracy is the key to successful piecing and making sure that the pixels stay horizontally and vertically aligned.

■ Only the cut widths are shown in the diagrams for clarity purposes. Heights are not given because *all* strips are cut 1½″ high.

■ When no width is given, use a 1½″-wide piece.

■ You do not need to backstitch when assembling the strips. Seamlines will be crossed by another seam, which will anchor them.

■ Keep a ruler handy to double-check the length of the pieces as you use them. While it's easy to differentiate a 1½″ piece from a 2½″ piece by simply looking at it, it's not quite as easy when you're trying to find the 22½″ piece instead of the 23½″ piece. It's easier to double-check the measurement now rather than having to rip apart an entire strip during Step 3: Quilt Top Assembly (page 10).

■ Use a blank piece of paper to help keep your place in the pattern diagram and underline the strip you are working on. Hold the paper in place with a small rotary cutting ruler or scissors.

■ If you're feeling overwhelmed by the chain piecing at any point, set out all of the pieces for the strip in the proper order. This will help keep your place in the strip while sewing.

■ Pin a small piece of paper with the number of the strip if you need help keeping track of the order of the strips.

■ If you need extra workspace at any point in the piecing, lower your ironing board to table height and set it next to your sewing machine. You can also store extra strips folded up on baking sheets.

STEP 3: quilt top assembly

1. When all the strips in the first section are complete, sew the strips together to form the first section and press.

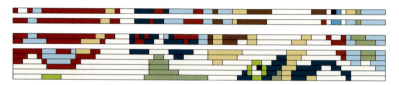

2. Assemble the next set of strips, and then sew them together to complete the second section. Repeat this step until all of the sections are complete.

3. Sew the completed sections together and press.

Quilt Top Assembly Notes

■ Remember to sew accurate ¼″ seams when sewing the rows together, so that the quilt doesn't end up skewed.

■ Backstitch to secure the seams at the beginning and end when sewing two strips together. There's no need to press the seams to the side in this step unless you love ironing. If you do, press the seams in the first strip all in one direction and then press in the opposite direction for the next strip.

■ A walking foot can help keep the strips aligned when sewing the strips together, but it's not guaranteed to be foolproof. Make sure to match up the intersections of the pixels as you sew.

Intersection

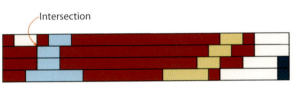

■ If there are no intersections to line up as you sew two strips together, use pins to keep the vertical alignment true.

■ Make sure not to pull the fabric when pressing, especially at the top and bottom of the quilt. Press lightly in an up-and-down motion. Avoid using a very hot iron or over-ironing, which can distort the pixels and strips.

■ While it's best to press the long seams open, it's also a monumental undertaking that I'm not sure many will want to take on. For most quilts, pressing to one side will be just fine.

■ Mistakes happen very easily in these quilts. Take your time to make sure you are using the right color, length, placement, and so on; and don't get frustrated if you end up having to rip out a strip or two to fix a misplaced pixel—it's happened to all of us.

STEP 4: quilting and finishing

BACKING

Make the backing a minimum of 8″ longer and wider than the quilt top. Piece, if necessary. Trim off the selvages before you piece to the desired size.

BATTING

The type of batting to use is a personal decision; consult your local quilt shop for help. Cut batting approximately 8″ longer and wider than your quilt top. Note that your batting choice will affect how much quilting is necessary for the quilt. Check the manufacturer's instructions to see how far apart the quilting lines can be.

LAYERING

Spread the backing wrong side up and tape the edges down with masking tape. (If you are working on carpet, you can use T-pins to secure the backing to the carpet.) Center the batting on top, smoothing out any folds. Place the quilt top right side up on top of the batting and backing, making sure it is centered.

BASTING

Basting keeps the quilt "sandwich" layers from shifting while you are quilting.

If you plan to machine quilt, pin baste the quilt layers together with safety pins placed a minimum of 3″–4″ apart. Begin basting in the center and move toward the edges first in vertical, then horizontal, rows. Try not to pin directly on the intended quilting lines.

If you plan to hand quilt, baste the layers together with thread using a long needle and light-colored thread. Knot one end of the thread. Using stitches approximately the length of the needle, begin in the center and move out toward the edges in vertical and horizontal rows, approximately 4″ apart. Add 2 diagonal rows of basting to form a big X across the quilt.

QUILTING

The main advice I have for quilting a pixel-based quilt is to *keep it simple.* It can be tempting to use several different thread colors to highlight this and outline that. These are already very busy quilts and need simplicity with a neutral thread that will blend into the fabrics. Before finalizing your plan, check your batting manufacturer's recommendations for how close the quilting lines must be.

Five Types of Quilting That Will Work with Any Pixel Quilt

Photo by Emily Cier

All five of these quilting designs will look fabulous on any pixel-based quilt and can be done on your home machine. Use a ruler and water-soluble pen, where needed, to draw stitching lines if the quilt doesn't have enough seams to follow.

Photos by Emily

Pixel grid   Start by quilting in-the-ditch along the long, strip seams. Stitch the vertical lines in the second pass.

Echo lines   Remember to keep it simple and not echo too many elements.

Stipple   You can't go wrong with this timeless classic.

Lattice   Crosshatch quilting at 45° angles is clean and simple.

Wacky lattice   Similar to Lattice but a little crazy. Wacky lattice requires no measuring and no straight lines.

Pantograph options

Having a longarmer quilt your pixel quilt is also an option. Here are some of the designs we used for the larger quilts in this book.

Photos by Emily Cier

BINDING

After the quilting is completed, trim off excess batting and backing even with the edges of the quilt top. A double-fold binding will work well for a pixel quilt.

Note

The given finished measurements of each quilt in Pixel Play do not include binding. Using the double-fold binding method (below) will add approximately ¼″ to each side of the quilt. For example, the Alki Throw quilt (page 36) measures 60″ × 60″. After the binding is added, the finished measurement will be 60½″ × 60½″.

Double-Fold Straight-Grain Binding

1. If you want a ¼″ finished binding, cut the binding strips 2½″ wide and piece them together with diagonal seams to make a continuous binding strip. Trim the seam allowance to ¼″. Press the seams open.

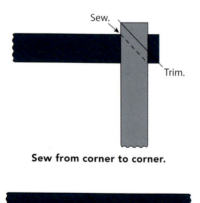

Sew from corner to corner.

Completed diagonal seam

2. Press the entire strip in half lengthwise with wrong sides together. With raw edges even, pin the binding to the front edge of the quilt a few inches away from the corner, and leave the first few inches of the binding unattached. Start sewing, using a ¼″ seam allowance.

3. Stop ¼″ from the first corner (Step A) and backstitch one stitch. Lift the presser foot and needle. Rotate the quilt one-quarter turn. Fold the binding at a right angle so that it extends

straight above the quilt and the fold forms a 45° angle in the corner (Step B). Then bring the binding strip down even with the edge of the quilt (Step C). Begin sewing at the folded edge. Repeat in the same manner at all corners.

Step A: Stitch to ¼″ from corner.

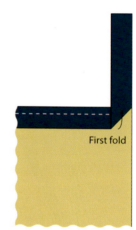

Step B: First fold for miter

Step C: Second fold alignment

Continue stitching until you are back near the beginning of the binding strip. See Finishing the Binding Ends (next page) for tips on finishing and hiding the raw edges of the ends of the binding.

Finishing the Binding Ends

METHOD 1

After stitching around the quilt, fold under the beginning tail of the binding strip ¼˝ so that the raw edge will be inside the binding after it is turned to the back of the quilt. Place the end tail of the binding strip over the beginning folded end. Continue to attach the binding and stitch slightly beyond the starting stitches. Trim the excess binding. Fold the binding over the raw edges to the quilt back and hand stitch, mitering the corners.

METHOD 2

See the tip "Completing a Binding with an Invisible Seam" at www.ctpub.com in the Consumer Resources section under Quiltmaking Basics.

Fold the ending tail of the binding back on itself where it meets the beginning binding tail. From the fold, measure and mark the cut width of your binding strip. Cut the ending binding tail to this measurement. For example, if your binding is cut 2½˝ wide, measure from the fold on the ending tail of the binding 2½˝ and cut the binding tail to this length.

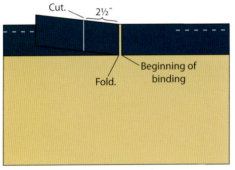

Cut binding tail.

Open both tails. Place one tail on top of the other tail at right angles, right sides together. Mark a diagonal line from corner to corner and stitch on the line. Check that you've done it correctly and that the binding fits the quilt; then trim the seam allowance to ¼˝. Press open.

Stitch ends of binding diagonally.

Refold the binding and stitch this binding section in place on the quilt. Fold the binding over the raw edges to the quilt back and hand stitch.

CRIB fishbowl

FINISHED SIZE: 40″ × 50″

Pieced and quilted by Emily Cier

This fishbowl is home to quite a variety of fish—but not to worry, they all get along quite grandly. In fact, they spend most of their time admiring each others' colors (and swimming in circles, naturally).

For a twin-size version of this project, see page 68.

YARDAGE

Letter	Yardage	Robert Kaufman Kona #–Color
A	1 yard	1037–Bone
B	½ yard	1072–Chartreuse
C	⅜ yard	1373–Teal Blue
D	⅓ yard	1479–Amber
E	⅓ yard	150–Paprika
F	⅓ yard	1282–Peacock
G	⅛ yard	1019–Black
H	¼ yard	1240–Mustard
I	¼ yard	275–Sable
J	¼ yard	1514–Robin Egg
K	⅓ yard	29–Spring
L	¼ yard	1064–Caribbean
M	⅛ yard	1386–Wheat
Binding	½ yard	1373–Teal Blue
Backing	2⅔ yards	1240–Mustard
Batting	48″ × 58″	

quilt assembly

1. Refer to One Strip at a Time: A Pixel Quilting Primer (pages 6–11) for assembly guidelines.

2. Assemble the quilt top using the assembly diagram (page 18).

3. Layer, quilt, and bind following the instructions in Quilting and Finishing (pages 11–15).

CUTTING

	A	B	C	D	E	F	G	H	I	J	K	L	M
First cut: Number of 1½″ × WOF strips to cut													
	22	8	7	5	6	5	2	4	3	3	6	3	2
Second cut													
23½″	1												
22½″	1												
15½″	1												
14½″	3										1		
13½″	4										1		
12½″	3												
11½″	5	1			1						1		
10½″	4	2						2			1		
9½″	3	1	1								2		
8½″	6	3	1	1	3			2			2		
7½″	5	1	1		2						2		
6½″	7		3	5	6	3		2		1	1		1
5½″	9	5	9	7	2	6		3		2	5		
4½″	21	4	9	2	7	2		1	1		6		1
3½″	22	7	8	11	10	11			2	3	6	3	
2½″	39	20	15	7	5	14		6	9	5	4	8	
1½″	34	51	17	5	5	4	7	2	21	13	4	13	2
Binding													
Cut 6 strips 2½″ × WOF.													

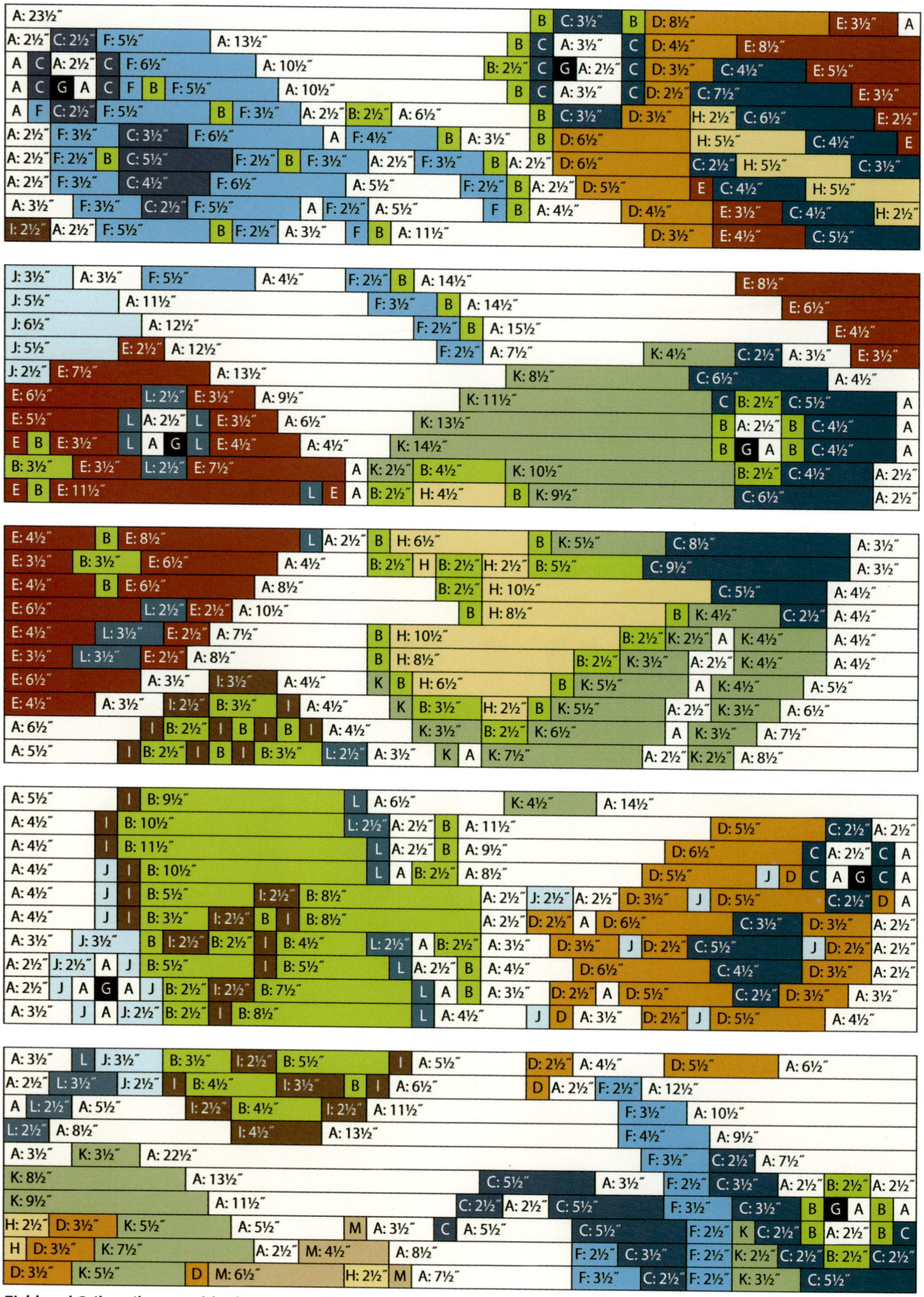

***Fishbowl* Crib quilt assembly diagram**

alternative palette

Dreaming of pastel-colored fish? Try this color combination (Robert Kaufman Kona #–color):

A: 1387–White

B: 1228–Melon

C: 318–Grapemist

D: 192–Mango

E: 1087–Coral

F: 24–Petunia

G: 1019–Black

H: 1481–Banana

I: 1484–Lupine

J: 1173–Ice Frappe

K: 21–Honey Dew

L: 1171–Hyacinth

M: 1003–Amethyst

Binding: 1484–Lupine

Backing: 1173–Ice Frappe

CRIB dithered

FINISHED SIZE: 43″ × 51″

Pieced and quilted by Emily Cier

We all know that rainbows result when sunlight strikes raindrops just so. But have you ever looked closely at those raindrops?

For a twin-size version of this project, see page 74.

	Letter	Yardage	Robert Kaufman Kona #–Color
YARDAGE	A	2⅓ yards	1037–Bone
	B	⅛ yard	274–Primrose
	C	¼ yard	355–Cayenne
	D	¼ yard	192–Mango
	E	¼ yard	23–Lemon
	F	¼ yard	351–Green Tea
	G	¼ yard	1084–Copen
	H	¼ yard	1484–Lupine
	Binding	½ yard	1084–Copen
	Backing	2⅞ yards	351–Green Tea
	Batting	51″ × 59″	

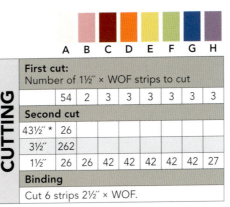

		A	B	C	D	E	F	G	H
CUTTING	**First cut:** Number of 1½″ × WOF strips to cut								
		54	2	3	3	3	3	3	3
	Second cut								
	43½″ *	26							
	3½″	262							
	1½″	26	26	42	42	42	42	42	27
	Binding								
	Cut 6 strips 2½″ × WOF.								

* For strips longer than 40″ wide, sew 2 strips together and then subcut the longer pieces.

quilt assembly

1. Refer to One Strip at a Time: A Pixel Quilting Primer (pages 6–11) for assembly guidelines.

2. Assemble the quilt top using the assembly diagram (page 22).

3. Layer, quilt, and bind following the instructions in Quilting and Finishing (pages 11–15).

Photo by Emily Cier

Photo by Emily Cier

Dithered Crib quilt assembly diagram

alternative palette

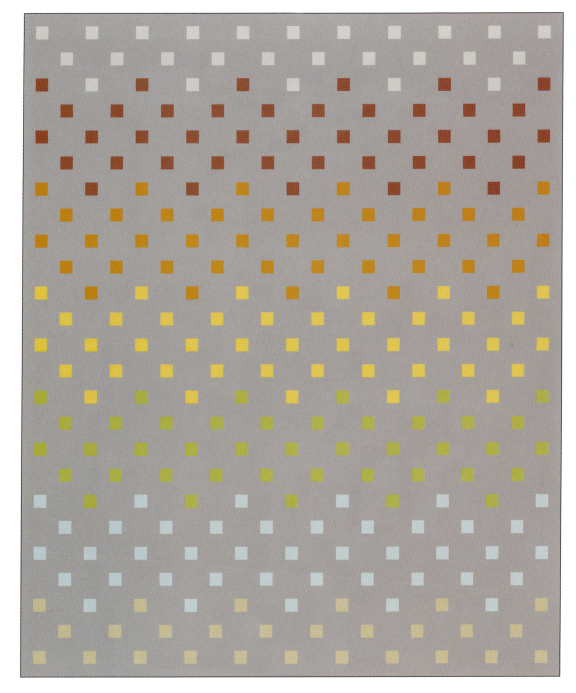

For a little boy, try this color combination (Robert Kaufman Kona #–color):

A: 1080–Coal

B: 1007–Ash

C: 1332–Sienna

D: 1479–Amber

E: 353–Sunflower

F: 347–Artichoke

G: 362–Dusty Blue

H: 1187–Khaki

Binding: 1479–Amber

Backing: 362–Dusty Blue

deception cove

FINISHED SIZE: 40˝ × 50˝

Pieced and quilted by Emily Cier

Avast! Is it land I see a'starboard? Aye, but we'll be in the hands of Davy Jones tonight if we don't look sharp and hold fast the rigging. For this is the site of Blackbeard's gold, and hazards wait unseen to foil us. Yarrr!

For a twin-size version of this project, see page 56.

Photo by Emily Cier

YARDAGE

	Letter	Yardage	Robert Kaufman Kona #–Color
	A	⅝ yard	1240–Mustard
	B	½ yard	1019–Black
	C	1 yard	194–Lake
	D	⅝ yard	199–Cactus
	E	⅛ yard	7–Tomato
	F	¼ yard	1362–Stone
	G	⅛ yard	1263–Olive
	H	⅛ yard	90–Pacific
	I	¼ yard	1703–Grass Green
	J	¼ yard	138–Earth
	K	¼ yard	1154–Gold
	L	¼ yard	1387–White
	Binding	½ yard	1240–Mustard
	Backing	2⅔ yards	1240–Mustard
	Batting	48″ × 58″	

CUTTING

	A	B	C	D	E	F	G	H	I	J	K	L
First cut: Number of 1½″ × WOF strips to cut												
	13	10	21	11	2	3	2	2	3	3	3	3
Second cut												
40½″ *	2											
25½″			1									
22½″	1		1									
19½″			3									
18½″			1									
16½″			1									
15½″			1									
14½″			2									
13½″	1		2	1					1			
12½″	2		2						1	1		
11½″			2	1								
10½″		1	6	2								
9½″	2		5	1								
8½″	1		5	3	2							
7½″		2	5	4								
6½″	1	1	7	5			1		1			1
5½″	1	5	5	4			1		1			
4½″	19	4	18	9			4	1	3			
3½″	19	6	20	19	1	5	2	1	5	1	3	6
2½″	31	22	28	21	3	10	3	5	5	1	9	6
1½″	31	121	30	24	2	2	5	5	3	16	9	1
Binding												
Cut 5 strips 2½″ × WOF.												

* For strips longer than 40″ wide, sew 2 strips together and then subcut the longer pieces.

quilt assembly

1. Refer to One Strip at a Time: A Pixel Quilting Primer (pages 6–11) for assembly guidelines.

2. Assemble the quilt top using the assembly diagram (page 27).

3. Layer, quilt, and bind following the instructions in Quilting and Finishing (pages 11–15).

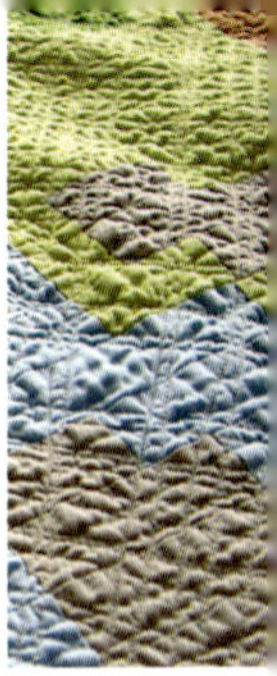

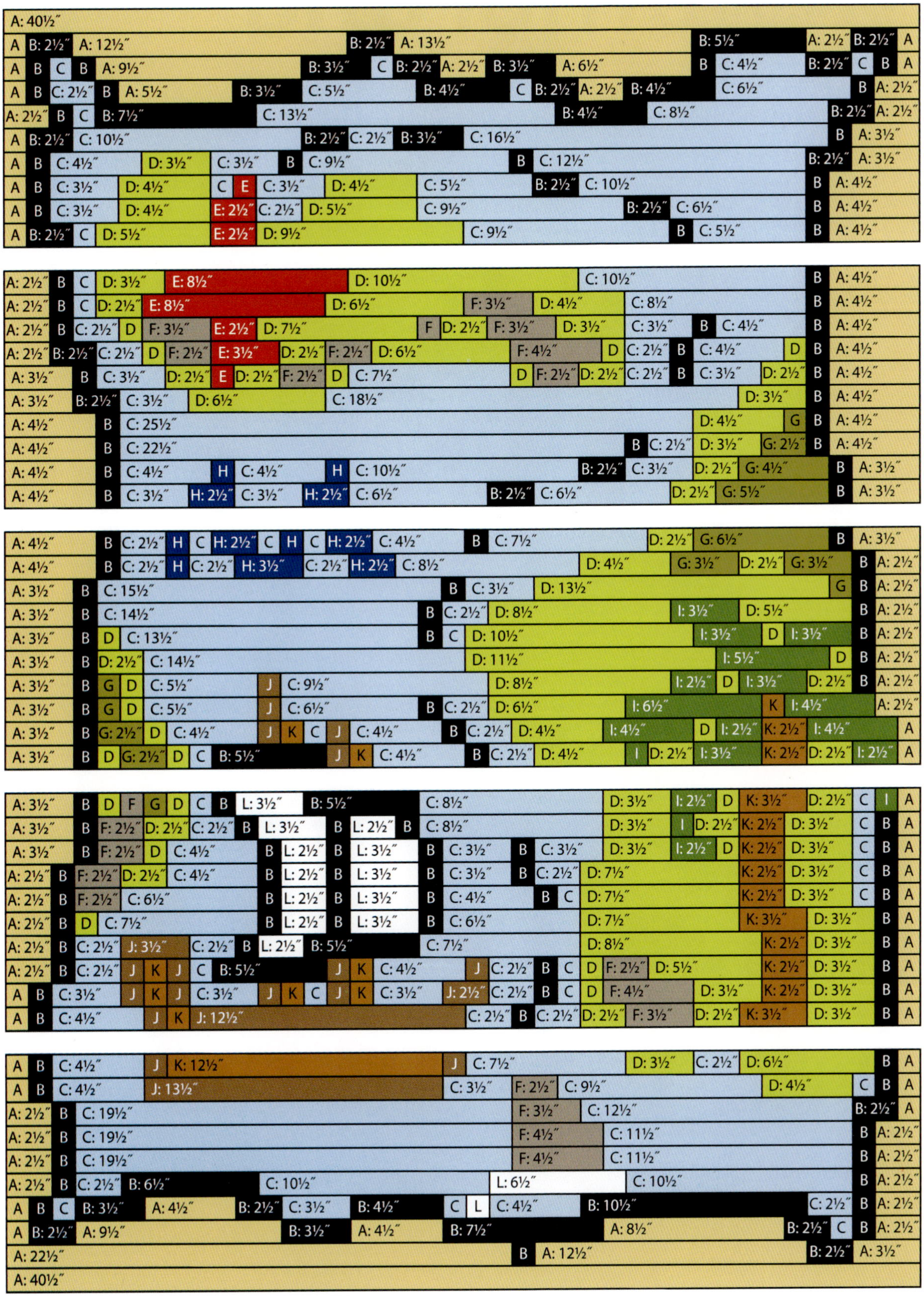

***Deception Cove* Crib quilt assembly diagram**

CRIB ambrosia

FINISHED SIZE: 40˝ × 50˝

Pieced and quilted by Emily Cier

If you're a butterfly, a flower's nectar is ambrosia. If you're this butterfly enjoying these flowers, well, all is right with the world.

For a twin-size version of this project, see page 64.

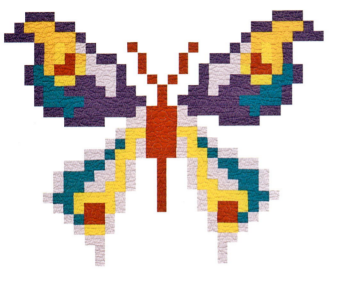

YARDAGE

	Letter	Yardage	Robert Kaufman Kona #–Color
	A	1⅜ yards	1055–Butter
	B	½ yard	142–Crocus
	C	¼ yard	149–Papaya
	D	¼ yard	1089–Corn Yellow
	E	¼ yard	24–Petunia
	F	¼ yard	7–Tomato
	G	⅓ yard	151–Cyan
	H	¼ yard	1514–Robin Egg
	I	¼ yard	1087–Coral
	J	¼ yard	1192–Lime
	K	⅓ yard	1703–Grass Green
	L	¼ yard	136–Basil
	Binding	½ yard	1192–Lime
	Backing	2⅔ yards	1055–Butter
	Batting	48″ × 58″	

Photo by Emily Cier

CUTTING

First cut: Number of 1½″ × WOF strips to cut											
A	**B**	**C**	**D**	**E**	**F**	**G**	**H**	**I**	**J**	**K**	**L**
31	8	3	4	4	3	5	3	4	3	5	3

Second cut	A	B	C	D	E	F	G	H	I	J	K	L
40½″ *	3											
24½″	1											
23½″	2											
21½″	1											
19½″	1											
18½″	1											
17½″	2											
15½″	3											
14½″	2											
12½″	2											
11½″	8											
10½″	5											1
9½″	6											
8½″	3							2				
7½″	5	2										
6½″	8	8							2			
5½″	10											2
4½″	24	4	2	4			4	4		1		
3½″	48	9	4	4	2	5	9	6	6		5	6
2½″	40	34	4	18	14	6	22	2	16	7	28	8
1½″	22	44	12	26	48	17	22	4	22	28	24	11
Binding												
Cut 5 strips 2½″ × WOF.												

For strips longer than 40″ wide, sew 2 strips together and then subcut the longer pieces.

quilt assembly

1. Refer to One Strip at a Time: A Pixel Quilting Primer (pages 6–11) for assembly guidelines.

2. Assemble the quilt top using the assembly diagram (page 31).

3. Layer, quilt, and bind following the instructions in Quilting and Finishing (pages 11–15).

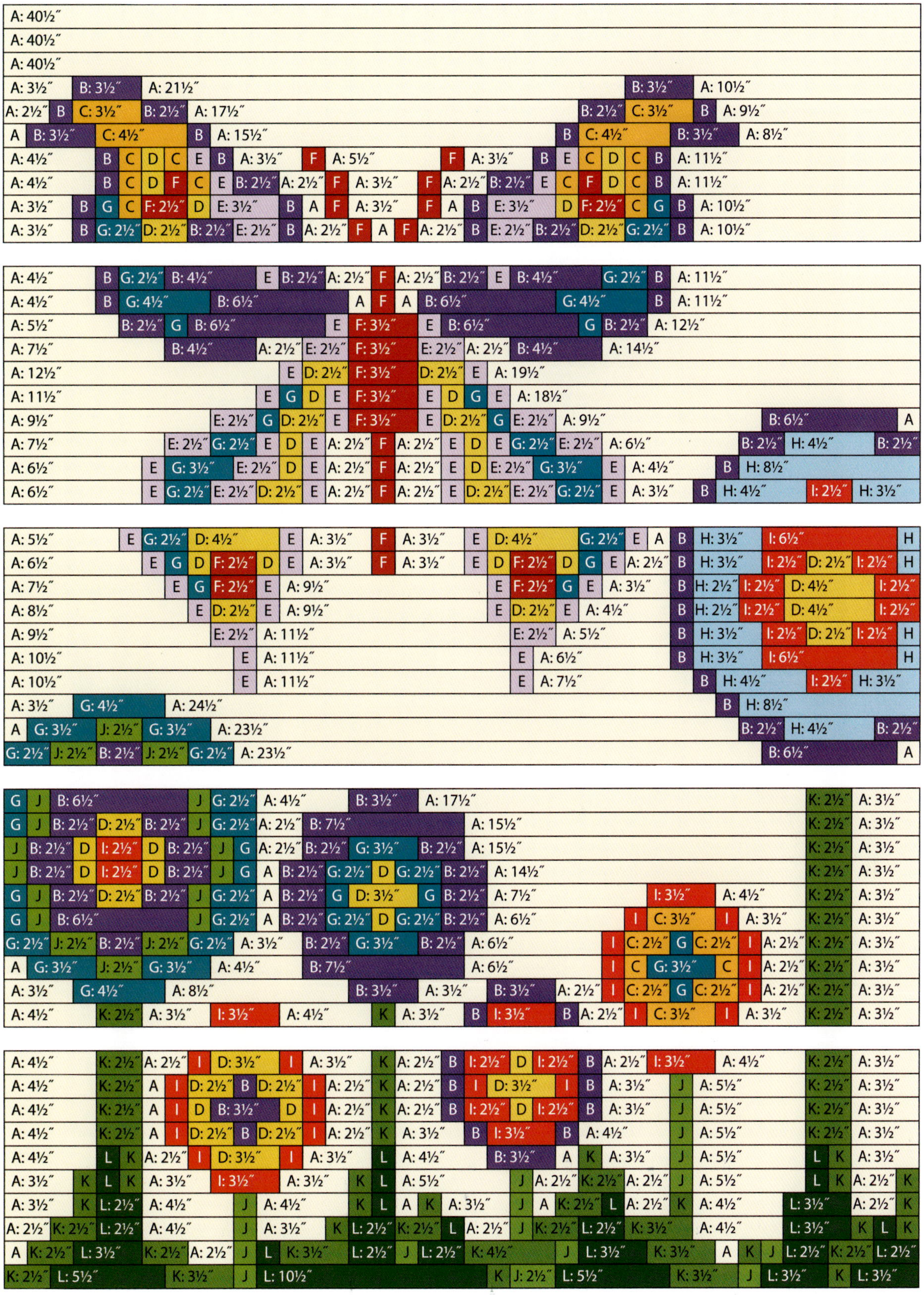
A: 40½″
A: 40½″
A: 40½″
A: 3½″ B: 3½″ A: 21½″ B: 3½″ A: 10½″
A: 2½″ B C: 3½″ B: 2½″ A: 17½″ B: 2½″ C: 3½″ B A: 9½″
A B: 3½″ C: 4½″ B A: 15½″ B C: 4½″ B: 3½″ A: 8½″
A: 4½″ B C D C E B A: 3½″ F A: 5½″ F A: 3½″ B E C D C B A: 11½″
A: 4½″ B C D F C E B: 2½″ A: 2½″ F A: 3½″ F A: 2½″ B: 2½″ E C F D C B A: 11½″
A: 3½″ B G C F: 2½″ D E: 3½″ B A F A: 3½″ F A B E: 3½″ D F: 2½″ C G B A: 10½″
A: 3½″ B G: 2½″ D: 2½″ B: 2½″ E: 2½″ B A: 2½″ F A F A: 2½″ B E: 2½″ B: 2½″ D: 2½″ G: 2½″ B A: 10½″
A: 4½″ B G: 2½″ B: 4½″ E B: 2½″ A: 2½″ F A: 2½″ B: 2½″ E B: 4½″ G: 2½″ B A: 11½″
A: 4½″ B G: 4½″ B: 6½″ A F A B: 6½″ G: 4½″ B A: 11½″
A: 5½″ B: 2½″ G B: 6½″ E F: 3½″ E B: 6½″ G B: 2½″ A: 12½″
A: 7½″ B: 4½″ A: 2½″ E: 2½″ F: 3½″ E: 2½″ A: 2½″ B: 4½″ A: 14½″
A: 12½″ E D: 2½″ F: 3½″ D: 2½″ E A: 19½″
A: 11½″ E G D E F: 3½″ E D G E A: 18½″
A: 9½″ E: 2½″ G D: 2½″ E F: 3½″ E D: 2½″ G E: 2½″ A: 9½″ B: 6½″ A
A: 7½″ E: 2½″ G: 2½″ E D E A: 2½″ F A: 2½″ E D E G: 2½″ E: 2½″ A: 6½″ B: 2½″ H: 4½″ B: 2½″
A: 6½″ E G: 3½″ E: 2½″ D E A: 2½″ F A: 2½″ E D E: 2½″ G: 3½″ E A: 4½″ B H: 8½″
A: 6½″ E G: 2½″ E: 2½″ D: 2½″ E A: 2½″ F A: 2½″ E D: 2½″ E: 2½″ G: 2½″ E A: 3½″ B H: 4½″ I: 2½″ H: 3½″
A: 5½″ E G: 2½″ D: 4½″ E A: 3½″ F A: 3½″ E D: 4½″ G: 2½″ E A B H: 3½″ I: 6½″ H
A: 6½″ E G D F: 2½″ D E A: 3½″ F A: 3½″ E D F: 2½″ D G E A: 2½″ B H: 3½″ I: 2½″ D: 2½″ I: 2½″ H
A: 7½″ E G F: 2½″ E A: 9½″ E F: 2½″ G E A: 3½″ B H: 2½″ I: 2½″ D: 4½″ I: 2½″
A: 8½″ E D: 2½″ E A: 9½″ E D: 2½″ E A: 4½″ B H: 2½″ I: 2½″ D: 4½″ I: 2½″
A: 9½″ E: 2½″ A: 11½″ E: 2½″ A: 5½″ B H: 3½″ I: 2½″ D: 2½″ I: 2½″ H
A: 10½″ E A: 11½″ E A: 6½″ B H: 3½″ I: 6½″ H
A: 10½″ E A: 11½″ E A: 7½″ B H: 4½″ I: 2½″ H: 3½″
A: 3½″ G: 4½″ A: 24½″ B H: 8½″
A G: 3½″ J: 2½″ G: 3½″ A: 23½″ B: 2½″ H: 4½″ B: 2½″
G: 2½″ J: 2½″ B: 2½″ J: 2½″ G: 2½″ A: 23½″ B: 6½″ A
G J B: 6½″ J G: 2½″ A: 4½″ B: 3½″ A: 17½″ K: 2½″ A: 3½″
G J B: 2½″ D: 2½″ B: 2½″ J G: 2½″ A: 2½″ B: 7½″ A: 15½″ K: 2½″ A: 3½″
J B: 2½″ D I: 2½″ D B: 2½″ J G A: 2½″ B: 2½″ G: 3½″ B: 2½″ A: 15½″ K: 2½″ A: 3½″
J B: 2½″ D I: 2½″ D B: 2½″ J G A B: 2½″ G: 2½″ D G: 2½″ B: 2½″ A: 14½″ K: 2½″ A: 3½″
G J B: 2½″ D: 2½″ B: 2½″ J G: 2½″ A B: 2½″ G D: 3½″ G B: 2½″ A: 7½″ I: 3½″ A: 4½″ K: 2½″ A: 3½″
G J B: 6½″ J G: 2½″ A B: 2½″ G: 2½″ D G: 2½″ B: 2½″ A: 6½″ I C: 3½″ I A: 3½″ K: 2½″ A: 3½″
G: 2½″ J: 2½″ B: 2½″ J: 2½″ G: 2½″ A: 3½″ B: 2½″ G: 3½″ B: 2½″ A: 6½″ I C: 2½″ G C: 2½″ I A: 2½″ K: 2½″ A: 3½″
A G: 3½″ J: 2½″ G: 3½″ A: 4½″ B: 7½″ A: 6½″ I C G: 3½″ C I A: 2½″ K: 2½″ A: 3½″
A: 3½″ G: 4½″ A: 8½″ B: 3½″ A: 3½″ B: 3½″ A: 2½″ I C: 2½″ G C: 2½″ I A: 2½″ K: 2½″ A: 3½″
A: 4½″ K: 2½″ A: 3½″ I: 3½″ A: 4½″ K A: 3½″ B I: 3½″ B A: 2½″ I C: 3½″ I A: 3½″ K: 2½″ A: 3½″
A: 4½″ K: 2½″ A: 2½″ I D: 3½″ I A: 3½″ K A: 2½″ B I: 2½″ D I: 2½″ B A: 2½″ I: 3½″ A: 4½″ K: 2½″ A: 3½″
A: 4½″ K: 2½″ A I D: 2½″ B D: 2½″ I A: 2½″ K A: 2½″ B I D: 3½″ I B A: 3½″ J A: 5½″ K: 2½″ A: 3½″
A: 4½″ K: 2½″ A I D B: 3½″ D I A: 2½″ K A: 2½″ B I: 2½″ D I: 2½″ B A: 3½″ J A: 5½″ K: 2½″ A: 3½″
A: 4½″ K: 2½″ A I D: 2½″ B D: 2½″ I A: 2½″ K A: 3½″ B I: 3½″ B A: 4½″ J A: 5½″ K: 2½″ A: 3½″
A: 4½″ L K A: 2½″ I D: 3½″ I A: 3½″ L A: 4½″ B: 3½″ A K A: 3½″ J A: 5½″ L K A: 3½″
A: 3½″ K L K A: 3½″ I: 3½″ A: 3½″ K L A: 5½″ J A: 2½″ K: 2½″ A: 2½″ J A: 5½″ L K A: 2½″ K
A: 3½″ K L: 2½″ A: 4½″ J A: 4½″ K L A K A: 3½″ J A K: 2½″ L A: 2½″ K A: 4½″ L: 3½″ A: 2½″ K
A: 2½″ K: 2½″ L: 2½″ A: 4½″ J A: 3½″ K L: 2½″ K: 2½″ L A: 2½″ J K: 2½″ L: 2½″ K: 3½″ A: 4½″ L: 3½″ K L K
A K: 2½″ L: 3½″ K: 2½″ A: 2½″ J L K: 3½″ L: 2½″ J L: 2½″ K: 4½″ J L: 3½″ K: 3½″ A K J L: 2½″ K: 2½″ L: 2½″
K: 2½″ L: 5½″ K: 3½″ J L: 10½″ K J: 2½″ L: 5½″ K: 3½″ J L: 3½″ K L: 3½″

***Ambrosia* Crib quilt assembly diagram**

CRIB pixelville

FINISHED SIZE: 40″ × 50″

Pieced and quilted by Emily Cier

Trains, planes, and automobiles! And buses, boats, bikes, and perhaps an occasional helicopter or motorcycle or skateboard. Good thing there are so many places to visit, because otherwise we wouldn't be able to have so much fun traveling between them!

For a twin-size version of this project, see page 60.

	Letter	Yardage	Robert Kaufman Kona #–Color
	A	½ yard	1703–Grass Green
	B	⅝ yard	316–Tarragon
	C	⅜ yard	1362–Stone
	D	⅜ yard	1080–Coal
	E	⅓ yard	26–Canary
	F	¼ yard	136–Basil
	G	⅓ yard	275–Sable
	H	¼ yard	7–Tomato
	I	⅛ yard	1007–Ash
	J	⅔ yard	1019–Black
	K	¼ yard	1060–Candy Blue
	L	¼ yard	1481–Banana
	M	¼ yard	1387–White
	N	⅛ yard	1016–Berry
	O	¼ yard	1005–Aqua
	P	⅛ yard	1479–Amber
	Binding	½ yard	1058–Cadet
	Backing	2⅔ yards	1362–Stone
	Batting	48″ × 58″	

YARDAGE

CUTTING

	A	B	C	D	E	F	G	H	I	J	K	L	M	N	O	P
First cut: Number of 1½″ × WOF strips to cut																
	8	13	7	7	5	4	6	4	2	14	3	3	3	2	4	2
Second cut																
31½″										1						
29½″				1												
28½″										1						
26½″				1												
24½″										2						
17½″			1													
14½″		2								3						
13½″		1													1	
12½″	1	2														
11½″		1	1							1					1	
10½″	1	1		4	1											
9½″	2	1	2		2										1	
8½″	1	2				1									1	
7½″	1	2								2			1		3	
6½″	3	3					2				2				1	
5½″	4	9		3		3		6		11			1		1	2
4½″	3	14	1			2	4			4		4	1		1	
3½″	11	15			10	1	1				1	6				
2½″	27	40	28	3	17	8	11			54			1		2	
1½″	35	40	55	52	36	18	77	42	14	57	21	4	20	9	1	
Binding																
Cut 5 strips 2½″ × WOF.																

quilt assembly

1. Refer to One Strip at a Time: A Pixel Quilting Primer (pages 6–11) for assembly guidelines.

2. Assemble the quilt top using the assembly diagram (page 35).

3. Layer, quilt, and bind following the instructions in Quilting and Finishing (pages 11–15).

Welcome to Pixelville!

Personalize your quilt by embroidering the town name in black within the welcome sign (color P).

Pixelville Crib quilt assembly diagram

THROW alki

FINISHED SIZE: 60″ × 60″

Pieced by Emily Cier and quilted by Cathy Kirk

If there's anything cheerier than a brightly colored bumbershoot on a stormy April afternoon, it's the chance to splash merrily in puddles—and then curl up under a warm quilt once you get home and dry off. Can you imagine anything other than a joyful grin hidden under that oversized umbrella?

YARDAGE

Letter	Yardage	Robert Kaufman Kona #–Color	Letter	Yardage	Robert Kaufman Kona #–Color
A	½ yard	1123–Dresden Blue	M	¼ yard	80–Mulberry
B	½ yard	1336–Slate	N	⅓ yard	347–Artichoke
C	⅜ yard	1029–Blue Bell	O	¼ yard	1706–Celery
D	⅓ yard	26–Canary	P	⅝ yard	362–Dusty Blue
E	⅜ yard	1072–Chartreuse	Q	⅝ yard	1513–Sky
F	⅓ yard	1064–Caribbean	R	⅓ yard	277–Blueberry
G	⅓ yard	1482–School Bus	S	⅝ yard	1010–Baby Blue
H	½ yard	165–Ivy	T	⅛ yard	1373–Teal Blue
I	¼ yard	1387–White	Binding	⅝ yard	1336–Slate
J	⅛ yard	1484–Lupine	Backing	3⅞ yards	1029–Blue Bell
K	¼ yard	1263–Olive	Batting	68″ × 68″	
L	¼ yard	134–Thistle			

CUTTING

First cut: Number of 1½″ × WOF strips to cut

	A	B	C	D	E	F	G	H	I	J	K	L	M	N	O	P	Q	R	S	T
First cut	10	8	7	6	7	6	5	8	4	2	4	3	4	5	4	11	11	6	13	2

Second cut

	A	B	C	D	E	F	G	H	I	J	K	L	M	N	O	P	Q	R	S	T
35½″																			1	
33½″																	1			
30½″							1													
29½″																1			1	
27½″																1				
26½″																			1	
24½″	1		1													1				
23½″																1				
22½″			3					1											1	
21½″			1													1				
20½″			1											1						
19½″				1				1												
18½″		1		1	1														1	
17½″					1					2				1		2	3			
16½″				1	2											1	1	1	1	
15½″	2	1		1	1															
14½″		1	1		2			2		1				1			2	1	6	
13½″					1			2						1	1	8	2		2	
12½″	3	1	1	1	1			1		1						2	2	2	3	
11½″	2	1	3		1	2		1						1		2	3		3	
10½″	4		1	1	1	3		2						1	1	2	1	2	1	
9½″	3	3			1	4										1		1	4	
8½″	2	4	1	1		2								1	1	3	3	3		
7½″	3	5	4	1	2	2	9	2		1	1			1	2	2	3	2		
6½″	2	3	3			4	7	2				3				1	2	1	1	
5½″	5	2	3	1	1	1	3	1			1	2				3	3	2	6	
4½″	9	2	1		1	3	1	2			1	6		1		3	4	1	5	
3½″	2	5	3	1	1	3	1	6	10	3	1		24	2	1	6	1	2	2	4
2½″	6	5	2		1	3	2	5	3	6	1	2	4	2		13	5	4	4	1
1½″	5	6	2		1	2		1	41	2		1	17	2		3	4	4	2	

Binding

Cut 7 strips 2½″ × WOF.

quilt assembly

37

1. Refer to One Strip at a Time: A Pixel Quilting Primer (pages 6–11) for assembly guidelines.

2. Assemble the quilt top using the assembly diagram (pages 38 and 39).

3. Layer, quilt, and bind following the instructions in Quilting and Finishing (pages 11–15).

Alki Throw quilt assembly diagram

Alki **Throw quilt assembly diagram**

THROW americana

FINISHED SIZE: 66″ × 60″

Pieced by Emily Cier and quilted by Cathy Kirk

Welcome to the neighborhood. There's a barbecue going on out back, and the mailman will likely be coming by any minute now. We've trimmed the trees and fluffed the clouds for your visit. Please don't pick the flowers, and we suggest you avoid discussing politics and homeowner's associations.

YARDAGE

Letter	Yardage	Robert Kaufman Kona #–Color		Letter	Yardage	Robert Kaufman Kona #–Color
A	1¼ yards	1028–Blue		K	⅓ yard	110–Peony
B	1⅛ yards	1387–White		L	¼ yard	1101–Delft
C	⅓ yard	1007–Ash		M	⅛ yard	362–Dusty Blue
D	½ yard	351–Green Tea		N	⅛ yard	1016–Berry
E	⅓ yard	317–Peridot		O	⅛ yard	149–Papaya
F	½ yard	1083–Coffee		P	⅛ yard	1484–Lupine
G	¼ yard	136–Basil		Q	⅜ yard	1362–Stone
H	⅝ yard	138–Earth		Binding	⅝ yard	1101–Delft
I	½ yard	275–Sable		Backing	3⅞ yards	1028–Blue
J	⅜ yard	1481–Banana		Batting	74″ × 68″	

CUTTING

First cut: Number of 1½″ × WOF strips to cut

	A	B	C	D	E	F	G	H	I	J	K	L	M	N	O	P	Q
	27	25	6	8	6	9	3	10	11	7	5	4	2	2	2	2	7

Second cut

	A	B	C	D	E	F	G	H	I	J	K	L	M	N	O	P	Q
66½″ *	1			1													3
49½″ *	1																
39½″	1																
35½″	1																
32½″	1																
30½″	1							4	1								
29½″	2	2															
28½″	1	1							5	1							
26½″								3									
24½″	3																
22½″	1	1						1									
21½″	2							1									
20½″	1	4						1									
19½″		1						1									
18½″	4							1	1								
17½″	1	4							1								
16½″	3	3							1	1							
15½″	3	2		2													
14½″		3									1						
13½″									2								
12½″	1	1															
11½″	1	1								2							
10½″	1	1	1														1
9½″	1	4			1												
8½″	3	5	2	2							2						
7½″	2	7		2	3			1	2								
6½″	1	6	3	5	1	1		1	1	1	1						1
5½″	2	6	1	2	2	6		1	1	3							
4½″	13	15	8		5	8	1	1	3	3	2	3					1
3½″	11	18	5	7	8	29	4	1	7	5	2	5					
2½″	37	10	17	16	14	17	9	1	10	4	5	5	14				
1½″	32	85	14	28	38	58	7	1	24	54	48	33		24	10	16	

Binding

Cut 7 strips 2½″ × WOF.

* For strips longer than 40″ wide, sew 2 strips together and then subcut the longer pieces.

quilt assembly

1. Refer to the chapter One Strip at a Time: A Pixel Quilting Primer (pages 6–11) for assembly guidelines.

2. Assemble the quilt top using the assembly diagram (pages 42 and 43).

3. Layer, quilt, and bind following the instructions in Quilting and Finishing (pages 11–15).

Americana Throw quilt assembly diagram

Americana **Throw quilt assembly diagram**

THROW snowflakes

FINISHED SIZE: 70˝ × 70˝

Pieced by Emily Cier and quilted by Cathy Kirk

Folks often say that no two snowflakes are alike, but frankly, no other snowflakes have ever been quite like these. Just be sure to make them well before the winter months hit, lest sewing these icy pixels makes for chilly fingers. Don't worry, the quilt won't melt.

YARDAGE

Letter	Yardage	Robert Kaufman Kona #–Color
A	1½ yards	362–Dusty Blue
B	4¾ yards	1339–Snow
Binding	⅝ yard	362–Dusty Blue
Backing	4⅓ yards	1339–Snow
Batting	78″ × 78″	

quilt assembly

1. Refer to the chapter One Strip at a Time: A Pixel Quilting Primer (pages 6–11) for assembly guidelines.

2. Assemble the quilt top using the assembly diagram (page 46).

3. Layer, quilt, and bind following the instructions in Quilting and Finishing (pages 11–15).

CUTTING

	A	B
First cut: Number of 1½″ × WOF strips to cut		
	33	108
Second cut		
55½″ *		1
53½″ *		1
40½″ *		3
39½″		2
36½″		2
35½″		2
34½″		3
33½″	1	
32½″		2
31½″		1
27½″		2
26½″		2
24½″		1
23½″		4
22½″		2
21½″		3
20½″		7
19½″		3
18½″		4
17½″		3
16½″		1
15½″		3
14½″		12
13½″		13
12½″		11
11½″	2	12
10½″		21
9½″	2	21
8½″	2	25
7½″		19
6½″	8	16
5½″	8	87
4½″	6	53
3½″	61	52
2½″	67	111
1½″	431	142
Binding		
Cut 6 strips 2½″ × WOF.		

* For strips longer than 40″ wide, sew 2 strips together and then subcut the longer pieces.

Snowflakes **Throw quilt assembly diagram**

alternative palette

For a dark and snowy night, try this color combination (Robert Kaufman Kona #–color):

A: 1387–White

B: 1223–Medium Grey

Binding: 1223–Medium Grey

Backing: 1223–Medium Grey

THROW zinnia

FINISHED SIZE: 65″ × 50″

Pieced by Emily Cier and quilted by Cathy Kirk

A field of fresh summertime wildflowers reminds you that the world is alive, but often a single blossom in its simplicity and delicate complexity is even more breathtaking. And that's even before you smell it.

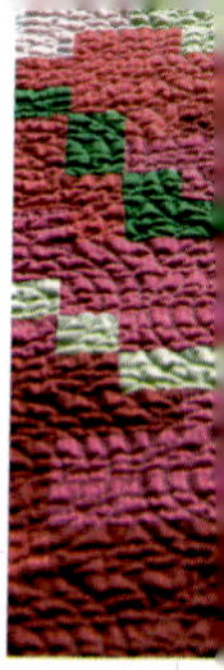

YARDAGE

Letter	Yardage	Robert Kaufman Kona #–Color	Letter	Yardage	Robert Kaufman Kona #–Color
A	¼ yard	359–Pepper	K	¼ yard	1237–Mocha
B	½ yard	147–Jungle	L	⅓ yard	1042–Brick
C	¾ yard	351–Green Tea	M	⅓ yard	1370–Tangerine
D	⅝ yard	1387–White	N	¼ yard	1216–Maize
E	⅝ yard	1145–Forest	O	⅓ yard	1045–Brown
F	⅜ yard	352–Ruby	P	¼ yard	1089–Corn Yellow
G	⅞ yard	1295–Pomegranate	Q	⅓ yard	1082–Cocoa
H	⅓ yard	1465–Dusty Peach	Binding	⅝ yard	1145–Forest
I	½ yard	1308–Red	Backing	3¼ yards	351–Green Tea
J	⅛ yard	149–Papaya	Batting	73″ × 58″	

CUTTING

	A	B	C	D	E	F	G	H	I	J	K	L	M	N	O	P	Q
First cut: Number of 1½″ × WOF strips to cut	4	8	15	12	12	7	18	6	9	2	3	5	5	3	6	3	5
Second cut																	
23½″			1														
22½″			1														
18½″			1														
17½″			1														
15½″			1														
14½″			1	1													
13½″			2	5													
12½″		1	1		1												
11½″		1	2		2		4										
10½″		5	1														
9½″		2	3		3		2										
8½″	1	1	3		4		4		1								1
7½″	1	2	3	1	3		6								1		1
6½″	3	3	4	9	6	2	5		1						1		
5½″	1	5	9	15	9	5	11	3	4		1						3
4½″	3	2	3	21	8	5	18	1	7			2			5		1
3½″	3	8	21	26	9	8	27	13	9	1	4	11	6	2	5		4
2½″	5	12	34	26	12	22	38	29	37	8	7	23	14	4	22	14	18
1½″	9	8	30	25	18	36	99	27	69	9	26	29	50	17	42	22	30
Binding																	
Cut 7 strips 2½″ × WOF.																	

quilt assembly

1. Refer to One Strip at a Time: A Pixel Quilting Primer (pages 6–11) for assembly guidelines.

2. Assemble the quilt top using the assembly diagram (pages 50 and 51).

3. Layer, quilt, and bind following the instructions in Quilting and Finishing (pages 11–15).

Zinnia Throw quilt assembly diagram

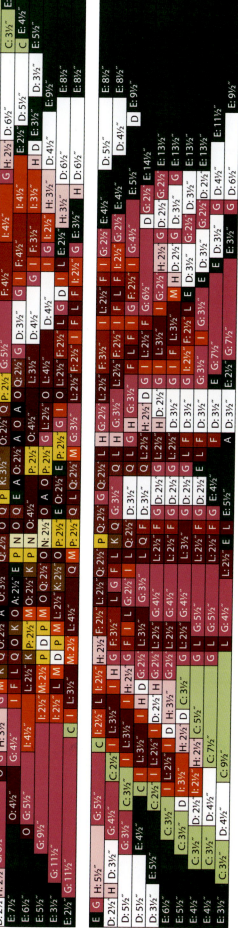

Zinnia **Throw quilt assembly diagram**

THROW clematis

FINISHED SIZE: 61″ × 61″

Pieced by Emily Cier and quilted by Cathy Kirk

Sometimes a little order amid the chaos is just what the doctor ordered, so this quilt gives you the lowest-maintenance formal garden you're likely to find. If you're tempted to make flower chains and go a bit hippie now and then—well, that's just fine too.

YARDAGE

Letter	Yardage	Robert Kaufman Kona #–Color
A	2¾ yards	184–Eggshell
B	⅝ yard	317–Peridot
C	½ yard	1058–Cadet
D	⅓ yard	1191–Lilac
E	½ yard	149–Papaya
F	½ yard	1087–Coral
G	⅝ yard	1133–Eggplant
H	½ yard	1011–Bahama Blue
Binding	⅝ yard	1058–Cadet
Backing	3⅞ yards	184–Eggshell
Batting	69″ × 69″	

CUTTING

	A	B	C	D	E	F	G	H
First cut: Number of 1½″ × WOF strips to cut								
	63	11	8	6	8	10	11	8
Second cut								
61½″ *	12							
45½″ *	1							
36½″	2							
31½″	1							
25½″	2							
24½″	2							
22½″	1							
20½″	5							
19½″	2							
18½″	2							
15½″	2							
14½″	5							
13½″	2							
12½″	2							
9½″	5							
8½″	5							
7½″	22							
6½″	17							
5½″	31	1						
4½″	27	6						
3½″	43	19	10	17	9			7
2½″	71	71	20	16	16	24	56	4
1½″	83	58	114	42	130	180	144	142
Binding								
Cut 7 strips 2½″ × WOF.								

* For strips longer than 40″ wide, sew 2 strips together and then subcut the longer pieces.

quilt assembly

1. Refer to One Strip at a Time: A Pixel Quilting Primer (pages 6–11) for assembly guidelines.

2. Assemble the quilt top using the assembly diagram (pages 54 and 55).

3. Layer, quilt, and bind following the instructions in Quilting and Finishing (pages 11–15).

Clematis Throw quilt assembly diagram

Block 1

A: 5½"	G	H	E: 3½"	H	G	A	B: 2½"	C	F	C	E: 3½"	C	F	C	A: 2½"	F	G	H	D: 3½"	H	G	F	A: 2½"	D	F	C	D: 3½"	C	F	D	A: 3½"	G	E	H: 3½"	E	G	B	A: 4½"
A: 2½"	B: 3½"	A	G: 2½"	E	G: 2½"	A: 4½"	C: 2½"	F: 2½"	E	F: 2½"	C: 2½"	A	B: 2½"	F	G: 2½"	D	G: 2½"	F	A: 3½"	D: 2½"	E: 2½"	D	E: 2½"	D: 2½"	A: 3½"	F	G: 2½"	H	G: 2½"	F	A: 5½"
B: 4½"	A: 3½"	G	H	G	A: 6½"	F	E	F	C	F	E	F	B: 3½"	A	H	E	G	H	G	E	H	A: 4½"	G	H	E	C	E	H	G	B: 5½"	H	G	E	G	H	A: 6½"
A: 2½"	B: 2½"	A: 4½"	G	A: 7½"	E	F	C	F	C	F	E	A	B: 2½"	A: 2½"	H	F	G	F	H	A: 5½"	H	G	D	F	D	G	H	A: 2½"	B: 2½"	A: 2½"	F	G	F	A: 7½"
A: 3½"	B	A: 14½"	G	A: 7½"	C: 3½"	A: 3½"	B: 2½"	A: 4½"	F	A: 9½"	D: 3½"	A: 4½"	B: 2½"	A: 12½"
A: 25½"	B	A: 22½"	B	A: 12½"
A: 61½"
A: 61½"
A: 7½"	D: 3½"	A: 25½"	B	A: 5½"	C	A: 9½"	C: 3½"	A: 5½"	B	A
A: 5½"	H	G	D	F	D	G	H	A: 7½"	G	A: 9½"	F	G	F	A: 3½"	B: 2½"	A: 2½"	H	C	G	C	H	A: 5½"	E	F	C	F	C	F	E	A: 2½"	B: 2½"	A

Block 2

A	B	A: 3½"	G	H	E	C	E	H	G	A: 6½"	G	H	G	A: 7½"	H	G	E	G	H	A: 2½"	B: 2½"	A	H	E	G	F	G	E	H	A: 4½"	F	E	F	C	F	E	F	A	B: 3½"	A
B: 3½"	A	D: 2½"	E: 2½"	D	E: 2½"	D: 2½"	A: 3½"	B	G: 2½"	E	G: 2½"	A: 2½"	B	A: 2½"	F	G: 2½"	H	G: 2½"	F	A	B: 3½"	C	G: 2½"	D	G: 2½"	C	A: 3½"	C: 2½"	F: 2½"	E	F: 2½"	C: 2½"	A: 2½"	B	A
A	B: 2½"	A	D	F	C	D: 3½"	C	F	D	A: 2½"	B	G	H	E: 3½"	H	G	A	B: 2½"	A	G	E	H: 3½"	E	G	B	A: 2½"	C	G	F	D: 3½"	F	G	C	A: 2½"	C	F	C	E: 3½"	C	F	C	A: 3½"	B
A: 2½"	B: 2½"	D: 2½"	E: 2½"	D	E: 2½"	D: 2½"	A	B: 2½"	A	G: 2½"	E	G: 2½"	A	B: 3½"	A	F	G: 2½"	H	G: 2½"	F	A: 4½"	C	G: 2½"	D	G: 2½"	C	A: 3½"	C: 2½"	F: 2½"	E	F: 2½"	C: 2½"	A: 3½"	B
A: 4½"	B	G	H	E	C	E	H	G	B: 4½"	A: 2½"	G	H	G	A: 4½"	B: 3½"	H	G	E	G	H	A: 5½"	H	E	G	F	G	E	H	B: 4½"	F	E	F	C	F	E	F	A: 5½"
A: 5½"	H	G	D	F	D	G	H	A: 3½"	B	A: 3½"	G	A: 9½"	F	G	F	A: 7½"	H	C	G	C	H	A	B: 2½"	A: 2½"	E	F	C	F	C	F	E	A: 5½"
A: 7½"	D: 3½"	A: 31½"	A: 3½"	B: 2½"	A: 4½"	C: 3½"	A: 7½"
A: 45½"	B	A: 15½"
A: 61½"
A: 36½"	B	A: 24½"

Block 3

A: 7½"	B	E	B: 2½"	A: 4½"	B	A: 13½"	C: 3½"	A: 3½"	B: 2½"	A: 14½"	D: 3½"	A: 7½"
A: 5½"	B	H	C	G	C	H	B: 2½"	A	B: 2½"	A: 2½"	F	G	F	A: 6½"	E	F	C	F	C	F	E	A	B: 2½"	A: 3½"	F	G	F	A: 6½"	H	G	D	F	D	G	H	A: 5½"
A: 4½"	B	H	E	G	E	G	E	H	A	B: 3½"	A	H	G	E	G	H	A: 5½"	F	E	F	C	F	E	F	B: 2½"	A: 3½"	H	G	E	G	H	A: 2½"	B: 3½"	G	H	E	C	E	H	G	A: 5½"
A: 3½"	B	A	C	G: 2½"	D	G: 2½"	C	A: 2½"	B	A	F	G: 2½"	H	G: 2½"	F	A	B: 2½"	C: 2½"	F: 2½"	E	F: 2½"	C: 2½"	B: 2½"	A	F	G: 2½"	H	G: 2½"	F	B: 2½"	A	D: 2½"	E: 2½"	D	E: 2½"	D: 2½"	A: 4½"
B: 3½"	A	E	G	E	D: 3½"	E	G	E	A: 2½"	B	G	E	H: 3½"	E	G	B: 2½"	A	C	F	C	E: 3½"	C	F	C	A: 2½"	B	G	E	H: 3½"	E	G	B: 2½"	A	D	F	C	D: 3½"	C	F	D	A	B	A: 2½"
A	B: 2½"	A: 2½"	C	G: 2½"	D	G: 2½"	C	A: 4½"	F	G: 2½"	H	G: 2½"	F	B: 2½"	A	C: 2½"	F: 2½"	E	F: 2½"	C: 2½"	A: 3½"	F	G: 2½"	H	G: 2½"	F	A	B	A	D: 2½"	E: 2½"	D	E: 2½"	D: 2½"	A	B: 2½"	A
A	B: 2½"	A: 2½"	H	E	G	E	G	E	H	A: 5½"	H	G	E	G	H	A: 2½"	B	A: 2½"	F	E	F	C	F	E	F	A: 5½"	H	G	E	G	H	A: 5½"	G	H	E	C	E	H	G	A: 2½"	B: 2½"	A
A	B	A: 4½"	H	C	G	C	H	A: 7½"	H	G	E	G	H	A: 2½"	B	A: 2½"	F	G	F	A: 6½"	E	F	C	F	E	A: 6½"	F	G	F	A: 6½"	H	G	D	F	D	G	H	B	A: 2½"	B: 2½"
A: 8½"	E	A: 20½"	C: 3½"	A: 19½"	D: 3½"	A: 3½"	B: 2½"	A: 2½"
A: 61½"
A: 61½"

TWIN deception cove

FINISHED SIZE: 76″ × 96″

Pieced by Emily Cier and quilted by Cathy Kirk

Pirate's maps, they say, were the key to leading the blaggards back to their own loot, so they would mark with care each sharp rock and hidden cove. But they would also use code and cunning to trip up anyone else who might find themselves in possession of the map and use it to find the rapscallion's hidden booty. So you can't be sure if that sea monster is truly a warning or instead a vital landmark—and whether those innocuous waves and inviting palms in fact mask the locations of treacherous rocks or unfriendly natives.

For a crib-size version of this project, see page 24.

YARDAGE

	Letter	Yardage	Robert Kaufman Kona #–Color
	A	1½ yards	1240–Mustard
	B	⅞ yard	1019–Black
	C	1⅞ yards	199–Cactus
	D	3¼ yards	194–Lake
	E	½ yard	1703–Grass Green
	F	⅔ yard	1263–Olive
	G	½ yard	1154–Gold
	H	⅓ yard	1362–Stone
	I	½ yard	90–Pacific
	J	¼ yard	7–Tomato
	K	¼ yard	138–Earth
	L	¼ yard	1387–White
	M	¼ yard	1479–Amber
	Binding	⅞ yard	1240–Mustard
	Backing	5⅞ yards*	1240–Mustard
	Batting	84″ × 104″	

* You may need additional backing fabric if your fabric is less than 44″ wide.

CUTTING

	A	B	C	D	E	F	G	H	I	J	K	L	M
First cut: Number of 1½″ × WOF strips to cut													
	33	18	41	75	9	14	8	6	8	3	3	4	3
Second cut													
76½″ *	3												
66½″ *	1												
51½″ *	1												
38½″				1									
35½″	1												
34½″				1									
33½″				1									
32½″				1									
31½″			1										
30½″				1									
28½″				2									
27½″				4									
26½″				1									
25½″				2									
24½″	1		1	2									
23½″				2									
22½″	1			1									
21½″	1			1									
20½″			1	5		2							
19½″				1		1							
18½″				6									
17½″			3	5									
16½″			1	7			1				1		
15½″	1		1	6		1					1		
14½″			1	6		2	1						
13½″		1	4	7		3							
12½″			6	6		1							
11½″	2		3	9		6							
10½″			8	18		2				2			
9½″	1	2	7	13		3							
8½″		1	9	20	1	3							
7½″	13	2	18	24	1	2							
6½″	15	6	16	14	1	4		1				1	2
5½″	20	2	30	17	7	6		4	4			2	
4½″	45	9	29	51	10	6	1	8	2			13	
3½″	35	13	57	54	16	13	18	18	10	1	1	2	4
2½″	34	49	68	48	37	9	62	15	51	6	2	3	4
1½″	33	235	65	72	27	13	17	4	45	2	22		8
Binding													
Cut 10 strips 2½″ × WOF.													

* For strips longer than 40″ wide, sew 2 strips together and then subcut the longer pieces.

quilt assembly

1. Refer to One Strip at a Time: A Pixel Quilting Primer (pages 6–11) for assembly guidelines.
2. Assemble the quilt top using the assembly diagram (pages 58 and 59).
3. Layer, quilt, and bind following the instructions in Quilting and Finishing (pages 11–15).

Deception Cove Twin quilt assembly diagram

Deception Cove Twin quilt assembly diagram

TWIN pixelville

FINISHED SIZE: *76″ × 96″*

Pieced by Emily Cier and quilted by Cathy Kirk

This dizzying town may seem to spend more time going from place to place than it does actually being in any one spot. But really, isn't that the point? I mean, what's the fun in sitting still when there are roads out there to explore?

For a crib-size version of this project, see page 32.

quilt assembly

1. Refer to One Strip at a Time: A Pixel Quilting Primer (pages 6–11) for assembly guidelines.

2. Assemble the quilt top using the assembly diagram (pages 62 and 63).

3. Layer, quilt, and bind following the instructions in Quilting and Finishing (pages 11–15).

Welcome to Pixelville!

Personalize your quilt by embroidering the town name in black within the welcome sign (color N). Enlarge the design below 150%.

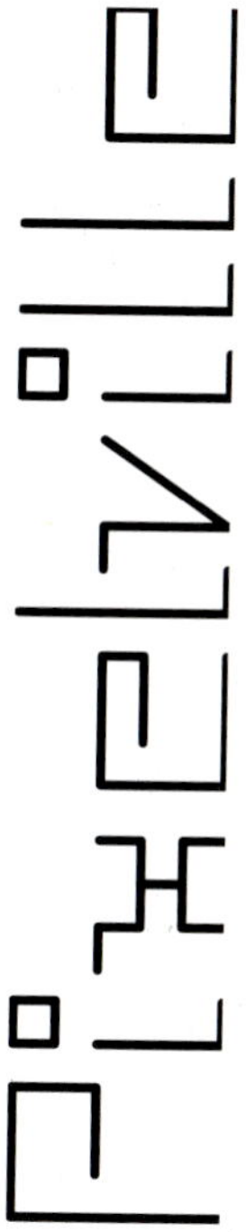

PIXELVILLE

YARDAGE

Letter	Yardage	Robert Kaufman Kona #–Color	Letter	Yardage	Robert Kaufman Kona #–Color
A	1½ yards	1703–Grass Green	K	¼ yard	1481–Banana
B	2⅔ yards	1019–Black	L	¼ yard	1007–Ash
C	⅞ yard	26–Canary	M	⅓ yard	1387–White
D	1¾ yards	316–Tarragon	N	¼ yard	1479–Amber
E	½ yard	1362–Stone	O	⅛ yard	1058–Cadet
F	½ yard	275–Sable	P	⅛ yard	1016–Berry
G	1¼ yards	1080–Coal	Q	⅓ yard	1005–Aqua
H	½ yard	136–Basil	Binding	⅞ yard	1058–Cadet
I	⅓ yard	7–Tomato	Backing	5⅞ yards*	1362–Stone
J	¼ yard	1060–Candy Blue	Batting	84″ × 104″	

* You may need additional backing fabric if your fabric is less than 44″ wide.

CUTTING

First cut: Number of 1½″ × WOF strips to cut	A	B	C	D	E	F	G	H	I	J	K	L	M	N	O	P	Q
	33	61	17	40	8	8	28	8	6	3	4	4	6	4	2	2	6
Second cut																	
51½″ *		1															
48½″ *		1															
42½″ *		4															
39½″		2															
38½″		2															
36½″		2															
31½″		4															
30½″		1															
29½″		1															
27½″		1															
26½″	1																
25½″	1			1													
23½″		2															
22½″				1													
21½″				1													
20½″		6		1			1										
18½″	1																1
17½″	1	6		1			1										
16½″	1			1	1												1
15½″	2			3			4	1									
14½″		1	1	1			6										
13½″		5		2			1										1
12½″	1		1	2			1	1									2
11½″	3	4		3									2				
10½″	5	1	1	7				1									2
9½″	3			8			7	2						2			2
8½″	2	2		11		1	14		1								3
7½″	6	4		17			31								1	1	2
6½″	11			12		2	1			2							1
5½″	15	62		18		1	11	3	6			2	7	3			2
4½″	35	7		27	1	5	14	6			4			1			2
3½″	72			36		6	44	10	3	1	13		2				2
2½″	72	241	109	96	43	30	2	28			3	3					3
1½″	110	171	191	170	65	85	88	24	94	21	14	65	80	33	18	13	1
Binding																	
Cut 10 strips 2½″ × WOF.																	

* For strips longer than 40″ wide, sew 2 strips together and then subcut the longer pieces.

Pixelville **Twin quilt assembly diagram**

Pixelville **Twin quilt assembly diagram**

TWIN ambrosia

FINISHED SIZE: 76″ × 96″

Pieced by Emily Cier and quilted by Cathy Kirk

Nectar is better when shared with a few good friends. These butterflies are so busy flitting and chatting that they're really not concerned that the flowers have decided to grow in every direction instead of constraining themselves to the traditional growth direction.

For a crib-size version of this project, see page 28.

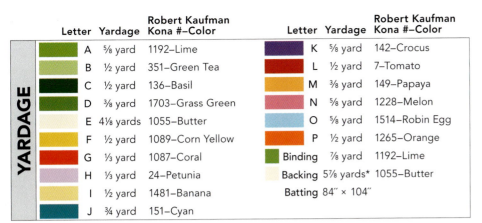

YARDAGE

Letter	Yardage	Robert Kaufman Kona #–Color
A	⅝ yard	1192–Lime
B	½ yard	351–Green Tea
C	½ yard	136–Basil
D	⅜ yard	1703–Grass Green
E	4⅛ yards	1055–Butter
F	½ yard	1089–Corn Yellow
G	⅓ yard	1087–Coral
H	⅓ yard	24–Petunia
I	½ yard	1481–Banana
J	¾ yard	151–Cyan
K	⅝ yard	142–Crocus
L	½ yard	7–Tomato
M	⅜ yard	149–Papaya
N	⅝ yard	1228–Melon
O	⅝ yard	1514–Robin Egg
P	½ yard	1265–Orange
Binding	⅞ yard	1192–Lime
Backing	5⅞ yards*	1055–Butter
Batting	84″ × 104″	

* You may need additional backing fabric if your fabric is less than 44″ wide.

CUTTING

	A	B	C	D	E	F	G	H	I	J	K	L	M	N	O	P
First cut: Number of 1½″ × WOF strips to cut																
	13	8	10	7	97	10	6	6	9	15	13	9	7	12	12	8
Second cut																
52½″ *					1											
37½″					1											
36½″					1											
35½″					1											
28½″					1											
25½″					1											
24½″					3											
21½″					3											
20½″					2											
19½″					2											
18½″					2											
17½″					10											
16½″					1											
15½″					10											
14½″					6							1				
13½″				1	8											
12½″		2			14											
11½″					24							1				
10½″					18											
9½″	1			2	27											
8½″					25	4		2					1		2	
7½″	2	1			32	2				4	2	2	3			
6½″	2	1	1		35	2	2	2	2		8	2				
5½″	3		4	2	58	13				10		3	5	4	2	3
4½″	3		10	3	62	6			4	4	4	2	4		8	6
3½″	12	5	24	5	95	24	12	12	17	20	18	17	15	16	22	5
2½″	57	34	37	31	89	16	30	20	48	48	54	33	19	78	20	25
1½″	124	64	55	37	37	38	30	50	52	174	116	59	30	102	136	78
Binding																
Cut 10 strips 2½″ × WOF.																

* For strips longer than 40″ wide, sew 2 strips together and then subcut the longer pieces.

quilt assembly

1. Refer to One Strip at a Time: A Pixel Quilting Primer (pages 6–11) for assembly guidelines.

2. Assemble the quilt top using the assembly diagram (pages 66 and 67).

3. Layer, quilt, and bind following the instructions in Quilting and Finishing (pages 11–15).

Ambrosia Twin quilt assembly diagram

Ambrosia **Twin quilt assembly diagram**

TWIN fishbowl

FINISHED SIZE: 76″ × 96″

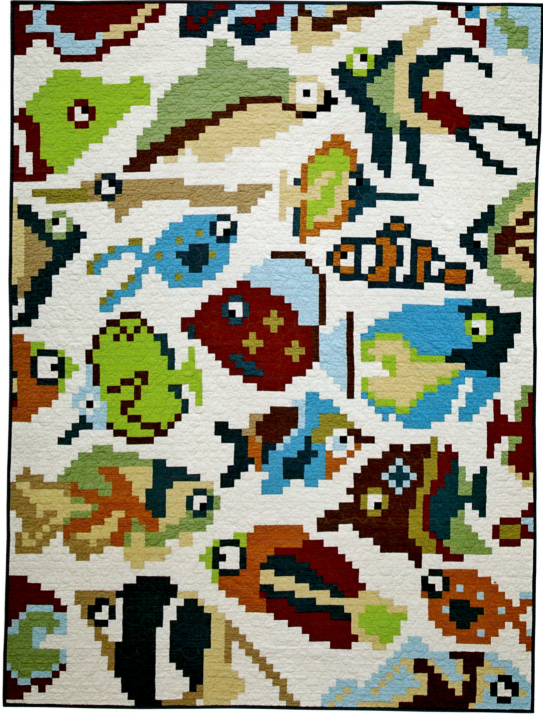

Pieced by Emily Cier and quilted by Cathy Kirk

You can find an even wilder collection of fish species in the wide open sea. In fact, it can get quite crowded at times—packed like sardines, if you will.

For a crib-size version of this project, see page 16.

Letter	Yardage	Robert Kaufman Kona #–Color
A	⅞ yard	150–Paprika
B	3½ yards	1037–Bone
C	⅝ yard	1514–Robin Egg
D	⅞ yard	1240–Mustard
E	1⅛ yards	1373–Teal Blue
F	⅝ yard	275–Sable
G	¼ yard	1019–Black
H	½ yard	1282–Peacock
I	⅝ yard	29–Spring
J	⅝ yard	1072–Chartreuse
K	⅝ yard	1479–Amber
L	⅓ yard	1064–Caribbean
M	½ yard	1386–Wheat
N	⅓ yard	1263–Olive
Binding	⅞ yard	1373–Teal Blue
Backing	5⅞ yards*	1240–Mustard
Batting	84″ × 104″	

YARDAGE

* You may need additional backing fabric if your fabric is less than 44″ wide.

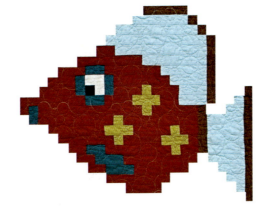

CUTTING

	A	B	C	D	E	F	G	H	I	J	K	L	M	N
First cut: Number of 1½″ × WOF strips to cut														
	17	80	12	19	23	12	3	10	12	13	11	6	8	5
Second cut														
30½″		1												
28½″		1												
27½″		1												
24½″		1												
22½″		1											1	
19½″		4												
18½″		3						1						
17½″		5						2	1					
16½″		7							1					
15½″		6											1	
14½″		6						1						
13½″	2	9			1			1	1					
12½″	1	10		2					2					
11½″	1	10	1	3				1		1				
10½″		13	1	2		1		1	1	3		1		
9½″	2	19	1	1	2	1		1	1	3	1	1		
8½″	5	27	2	3	3	1		1	3	4	2	2		1
7½″	11	34	3	2	3	2		1	1	4	2	1		
6½″	11	29	1	12	15	8		4	6	4	7		2	1
5½″	6	51	7	9	21	11		10	6	10	9	2	4	1
4½″	12	42	11	13	26	11		10	13	9	8	1	7	1
3½″	26	63	18	33	52	17		16	14	7	25	12	8	8
2½″	40	116	45	63	62	28	3	22	24	30	32	20	29	12
1½″	55	98	47	63	87	56	22	9	32	44	31	32	27	29
Binding														
Cut 10 strips 2½″ × WOF.														

quilt assembly

1. Refer to One Strip at a Time: A Pixel Quilting Primer (pages 6–11) for assembly guidelines.

2. Assemble the quilt top using the assembly diagram (pages 71 and 72).

3. Layer, quilt, and bind following the instructions in Quilting and Finishing (pages 11–15).

...hbowl Twin quilt assembly diagram—top half (continued on next page)

Fishbowl Twin quilt assembly diagram—bottom half (continued from previous page)

alternative palette

Dreaming of pastel-colored fish? Try this color combination (Robert Kaufman Kona #–color):

A: 1087–Coral

B: 1387–White

C: 1173–Ice Frappe

D: 1481–Banana

E: 318–Grapemist

F: 1003–Amethyst

G: 1019–Black

H: 24–Petunia

I: 1484–Lupine

J: 1706–Celery

K: 192–Mango

L: 1171–Hyacinth

M: 21–Honey Dew

N: 1228–Melon

Binding: 1484–Lupine

Backing: 1173–Ice Frappe

TWIN dithered

FINISHED SIZE: 79″ × 99″

Pieced by Emily Cier and quilted by Cathy Kirk

Some days, rainclouds give us dramatic, brooding thunderstorms or endless gray fog. Other times, though, they splash color into the world, and sheets of tiny droplets can brighten an entire day.

For a crib-size version of this project, see page 20.

Photo by Emily Ciel

YARDAGE

Letter	Yardage	Robert Kaufman Kona #–Color
A	8 yards	1037–Bone
B	⅜ yard	274–Primrose
C	⅜ yard	355–Cayenne
D	⅜ yard	192–Mango
E	⅜ yard	23–Lemon
F	⅜ yard	351–Green Tea
G	⅜ yard	1084–Copen
H	⅜ yard	1484–Lupine
Binding	⅞ yard	1084–Copen
Backing	6 yards*	351–Green Tea
Batting	87″ × 107″	

* You may need additional backing fabric if your fabric is less than 44″ wide.

CUTTING

	A	B	C	D	E	F	G	H
First cut: Number of 1½″ × WOF strips to cut								
	188	7	7	7	7	7	7	7
Second cut								
79½″ *	50							
3½″	955							
1½″	50	137	136	137	136	137	136	137
Binding								
Cut 10 strips 2½″ × WOF.								

* For strips longer than 40″ wide, sew 2 strips together and then subcut the longer pieces.

quilt assembly

1. Refer to One Strip at a Time: A Pixel Quilting Primer (pages 6–11) for assembly guidelines.

2. Assemble the quilt top using the assembly diagram (pages 76 and 77).

3. Layer, quilt, and bind following the instructions in Quilting and Finishing (pages 11–15).

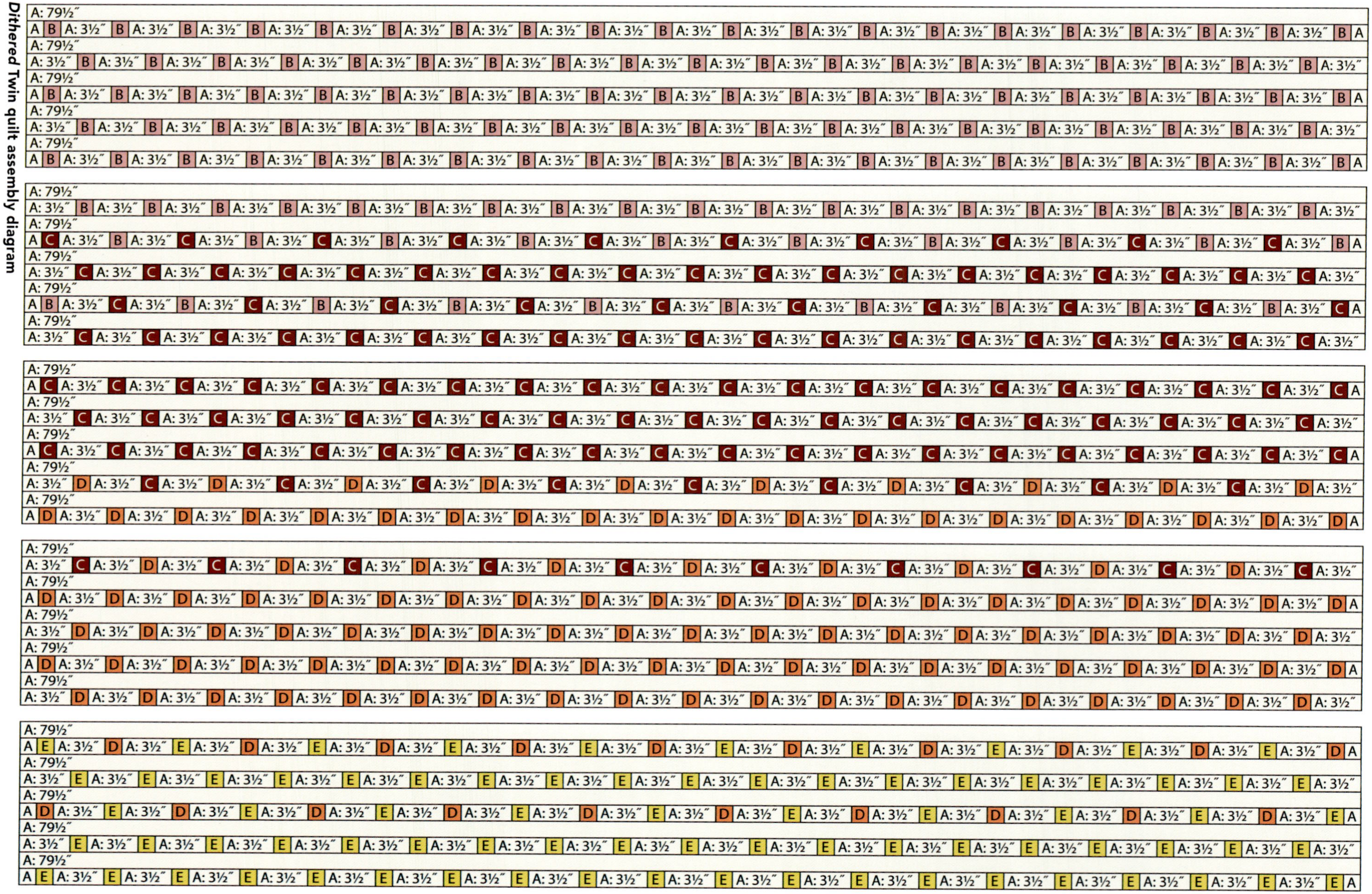

Dithered Twin quilt assembly diagram

Dithered Twin quilt assembly diagram

alternative palette

You mean your 13-year-old son doesn't want a quilt with green tea and primrose?
Try this color combination (Robert Kaufman Kona #–color):

A: 1080–Coal

B: 1007–Ash

C: 1332–Sienna

D: 1479–Amber

E: 353–Sunflower

F: 347–Artichoke

G: 362–Dusty Blue

H: 1187–Khaki

Binding: 1479–Amber

Backing: 362–Dusty Blue

resources

Visit www.robertkaufman.com for the complete palette of Robert Kaufman Kona Cotton Solids and a list of retail stores in your area.

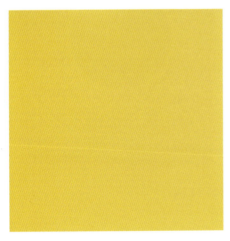

about the author

Emily Cier has had a lifelong love of fine art and art history and has a background in graphic design. These passions finally found a common ground in quilting, which she quickly discovered to be a wonderful and timeless creative outlet as well as one filled with a rich history. It also keeps one quite toasty on a cold, rainy day.

Emily lives in Seattle with her husband and two beautiful children, who are showing their own penchant for creativity.

For more of Emily's work, visit her website at www.carolinapatchworks.com.

Also by Emily Cier:

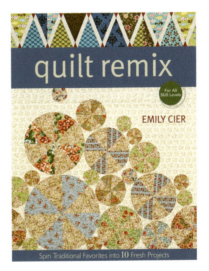

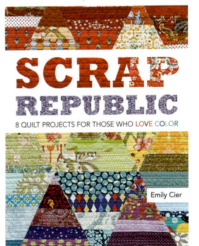

Great Titles and Products

from C&T PUBLISHING

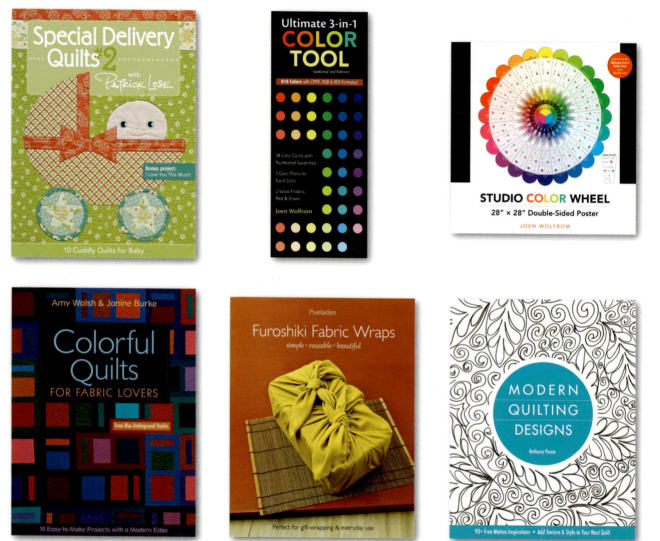

Available at your local retailer or **www.ctpub.com** *or* **800-284-1114**